Stylish
KNIT SCARVES & HATS
with Mademoiselle Sophie

Mademoiselle Sophie of
Breaking the wool

Paris — San Francisco

STACKPOLE
BOOKS

This translation of *Écharpes & Cie à Tricoter* first published in France by LIBELLA under the imprint LTA in 2014 is published by arrangement with Silke Bruenink Agency, Munich, Germany.

This edition published by STACKPOLE BOOKS, 5067 Ritter Road, Mechanicsburg, PA 17055, www.stackpolebooks.com

Editorial direction: Anne-Sophie Pawlas
Editing: Isabelle Riener
Proofreading: Annie Rage
Graphic design: Anne Bénoliel-Defréville
Pagination: Coline de Graaff
Cover design: Tessa J. Sweigert
Photography: Claire Curt
Styling: Sonia Lucano
Production: Géraldine Boilley-Hautbois, Louise Martinez
Photoengraving: Quadri Offset
Translation: Kathryn Fulton

Printed in the United States of America

10 9 8 7 6 5 4 3 2 1

First edition

Library of Congress Cataloging-in-Publication Data

Sophie, Mademoiselle.
  [Écharpes & cie à tricoter. English]
  Stylish knit scarves & hats with Mademoiselle Sophie : 23 beautiful patterns with child sizes too / Mademoiselle Sophie of Breaking the Wool.
    pages cm
  ISBN 978-0-8117-1607-9
  1. Knitting. 2. Scarves. 3. Hats. I. Title. II. Title: Stylish knit scarves and hats with Mademoiselle Sophie.
  TT825.S7131513 2015
  746.43'2—dc23
        2015017164

Preface

My earliest memories of knitting have the flavor of childhood. Sitting on my grandmother's lap, I watched one stitch after another slide across her needles. Magic before my eyes: simple balls of yarn transformed into big scarves, delicate cardigans, warm afghans, and magnificent and timeless shawls.

Several years later, my mother gave me my first balls of yarn and lent an ear to all my questions.

All of this was what inspired me to create Breaking the Wool, whose ambition is to make this ancestral practice, which many unfairly judge to be old-fashioned and boring, more modern and accessible.

I want to encourage you to use your needles always and everywhere; may the creations in this book inspire you! I also hope—why not?—to kindle a few vocations.

Mlle Sophie

Contents

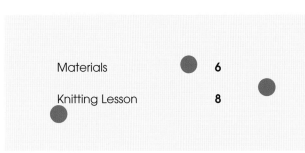

Materials

❊ Yarn

Use natural yarn, such as wool, alpaca, merino, and cashmere, when possible; but you can also use wool-acrylic or wool-mohair blends. Your choice of yarn depends on the project you're making, and is very important. Make it a priority to use materials that are soft and pleasant to work with; you'll be more eager to work on and wear your projects!

❊ Straight needles

Straight needles in sizes 6 (4.0 mm), 7 (4.5 mm), 8 (5.0 mm), 9 (5.5 mm), 10 (6.0 mm), 10½ (6.5 mm), 11 (8 mm), 13 (9 mm), and 17 (12.75 mm) are used in this book. A wide selection of knitting needles is available. My favorites are the bamboo ones, but they also come in metal, plastic, and wood.

The feeling of working with needles in different materials is very different; try several to find out which you prefer.

6

Use mohair and silk yarns for their softness.

❊ Circular needles

You will also need circular needles in sizes 6 (4.0 mm), 8 (5.0 mm), 9 (5.5 mm), and 17 (12.75 mm), all 16" (40 cm) long except the size 6 (4.0 mm) which is 32"/80 cm long. Used for knitting in the round without seams (sometimes called "magic loop"), and very easy to use, these needles can also be used for working back and forth in rows, like straight needles. (Note that when knitting in the round, you're always working on the right side.) Circular needles are indispensable for projects with so many stitches that they won't fit on straight needles. Very practical, they allow you to bring your knitting with you everywhere without taking up much space, thanks to the cable in the middle which bends easily.

There are different types of circular needles:
• fixed, which can be bought with different cable lengths;
• interchangeable, in which the cable detaches with the help of a little key. A cap can be screwed onto the end of the cable, allowing you to set your work aside.

❊ Stitch markers

Ring-style stitch markers are indispensable for marking a specific point on a piece, or for indicating the beginning and end of rounds for a piece worked on circular needles. The stitch marker can be slid onto the needle between two stitches. When you come around to it again, transfer it from one needle to the other to keep the marked location, then continue knitting.

Metallic yarn can give a project sparkle.

Knitting Lesson

CASTING ON

1. Make a slip knot, leaving a long tail of yarn, and place the loop around the needle. Wind the tail of the yarn around your left thumb, with the needle in your right hand.
2. Insert the point of the needle into the loop around your left thumb and, holding the needle with your left hand, wrap the working yarn (the end coming from the ball) around the point of the needle and draw it through the loop toward you.
3. Bring the loop over the point of the needle.
4. Gently pull down on the yarn end on the left: a stitch is formed on the needle. Repeat the process until you have as many stitches as the pattern calls for.

KNITTING

1. Start with the work in your left hand and the yarn to the back. Wrap the yarn around your right index finger. Insert the right needle into the first stitch, going under the left needle.
2. Wrap the yarn around the right needle, from bottom to top.
3. Bring the right needle down carefully, bringing the point through the stitch and back to the top of the left needle.
4. Drop the loop you just knit through from the left needle. You have created a new stitch on the right needle.
5. Repeat the process, stitch after stitch, so that all the stitches from the left needle are moved to the right needle; this will create a new row of stitches.

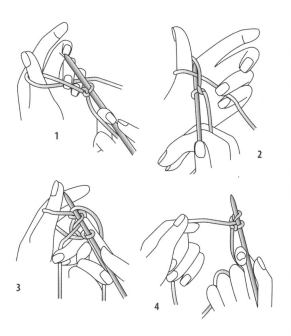

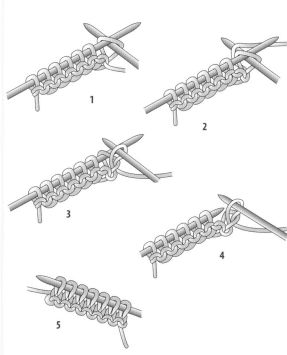

PURLING

1. Start with the yarn in front of the work. Insert the right needle into the first stitch on the left needle, with the right needle going on top of the left needle.
2. Wrap the yarn around the right needle.
3. Slide the right needle back underneath the left needle.
4. Gently pull on the left needle to drop the loop from it. You have created a new stitch on the right needle.
5. Repeat the process, stitch after stitch, so that all the stitches from the left needle are moved to the right needle; this will create a new row of stitches.

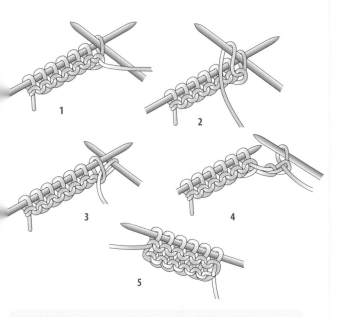

STOCKINETTE STITCH

Row 1: Knit every stitch.
Row 2: Purl every stitch.
Return to Row 1 and continue to repeat these two rows.
When working in the round, knit all stitches in every round.

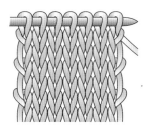

GARTER STITCH
Knit every row.

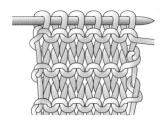

1 X 1 RIBBING

Row 1: Alternate one knit stitch and one purl stitch, making sure to bring the working yarn behind the work for each knit stitch and in front of the work for each purl stitch.
For the following rows, work each stitch the same as in the row before: knit into stitches when they appear as knit stitches and purl into those that appear as purl stitches.

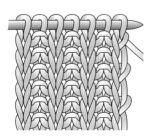

9

GAUGE

Making a sample swatch is essential for avoiding unpleasant surprises. A project may come out a very different size, the knitted fabric can end up loose (because the yarn would have worked better with a smaller needle), or a collar may end up too tight, depending on how tightly you knit. Only a gauge swatch will ensure your project matches the original sample. If the gauge swatch is larger than the given dimensions, use needles one size smaller; if the swatch is too small, try a size bigger.

SEED STITCH

Row 1: Alternate one knit stitch and one purl stitch (as with 1 x 1 ribbing, remember to bring the yarn to the front or back according to the stitch you're knitting).

Row 2: The stitches that appear as knit stitches should be purled, and those that appear as purl stitches should be knitted.

Return to Row 1 and continue to repeat these two rows.

KNIT 2 STITCHES TOGETHER

Insert the right needle into the second stitch on the left needle, then through the first stitch at the same time; then wrap and pull the yarn through the two stitches at the same time, just as if you only had one stitch on the needle.

YARN OVER

This is a way to add a stitch in order to form a small hole. Bring the working yarn over the right needle without knitting with it (1), then knit the next stitch normally (2); you should have one more stitch (3). To keep the number of stitches the same, knit two stitches together or work a slip, knit, pass (skp).

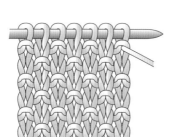

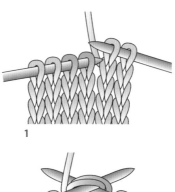

1

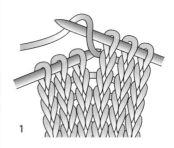

1

SLIP

Bring the yarn to the back, insert the right needle into the first stitch on the left needle, then slide it onto the right needle without knitting it.

2

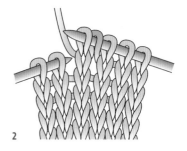

2

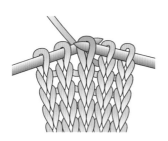

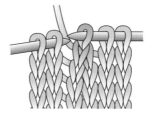

3

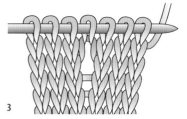

3

10

SLIP, KNIT, PASS

Slip one stitch knitwise from the left needle to the right needle (1), knit the next stitch normally, then pull the slipped stitch over the knit stitch (2). You will have one less stitch (3).

SIMPLE DECREASES OF 1 STITCH AT THE EDGES

Work two stitches together according to the kind of stitch they are: knit two knit stitches together or purl two purl stitches together.

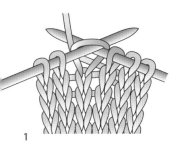

1

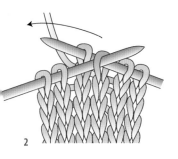

2

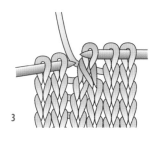

3

MAKE ONE INCREASE

When working a make one increase, pay attention to the slant—first right, then left—for each group of increases.

- **Make one right:** Use the right needle to pick up the strand of yarn between two stitches and place it on the left needle so that the yarn goes from the front of the needle to the back (1). Then insert the right needle into this loop, twisting it (2). Wrap the yarn around the right needle and knit through the loop: you have created a new stitch, slanted to the right.
- **Make one left:** Use the right needle to pick up the strand of yarn between two stitches and place it on the left needle so that the yarn goes from back to front (1). Insert the right needle into this loop from behind the left needle and slide it through toward the back (2). Wrap the yarn around the needle and knit through the loop: you have created a new stitch, slanted to the left.

CASTING ON MORE STITCHES

At the beginning of a row, knit one stitch, but do not pull it off the left needle. Place the stitch obtained on the left needle: you have added one stitch. Knit this stitch, again without pulling it off the left needle, and place the stitch obtained on the left needle, and so on, until you have the desired number of stitches.

BINDING OFF STITCHES

Knit the first two stitches, then insert the left needle into the first stitch, and draw this stitch over the second stitch and off the right needle (1). Knit a third stitch, then insert the left needle into the second stitch and draw it over the third stitch. Continue in this pattern, knitting one stitch at a time and binding off each stitch as you go. At the end of the row, there will be one stitch left (2); cut the yarn, draw the end through this remaining loop, and pull gently to fasten off.

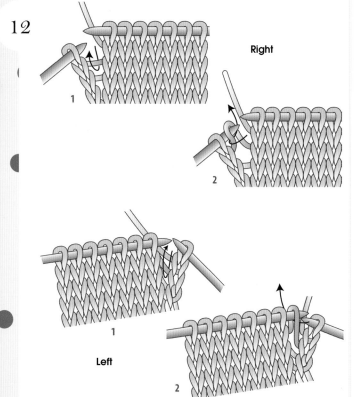

Right

Left

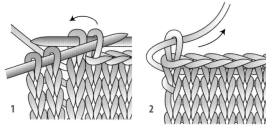

ASSEMBLING PIECES SIDE BY SIDE

For an attractive finish with invisible seams, first iron the pieces to be assembled so that the edges are nice and flat. Place them side by side, with the right sides facing you, and insert a threaded tapestry needle through the edge stitch of the first piece, then through the edge stitch of the second piece. Pull gently to join the two edges together for an invisible seam. Continue in this way until the seam is completed.

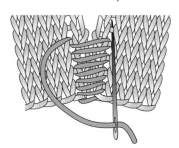

14

BLOCKING YOUR WORK

When a piece is completed, blocking will give it a good finish; it will gently flatten the piece and certain stitches, such as edges and cables, will be highlighted. Gently iron all the pieces on the wrong side. If some edges have a tendency to curl up, iron them a second time, very gently, on the right side. Then assemble the whole piece.

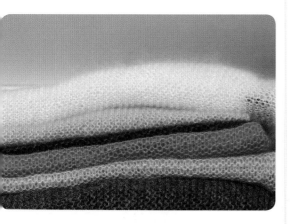

SOME TIPS

• When you start a skein of yarn, it's best to use the end on the outside of the skein for fine yarns, and the end from the inside of the skein for thicker yarns; this way the skein will unwind easily. To change from one skein to another, make the splice over three stitches next to the edge of the piece. Knit with the old yarn and the new yarn at the same. Don't make a knot.

• To achieve an even knit, practice on smaller pieces (doll scarves or squares for a small afghan). The yarn must be knitted smoothly—not too loose, not too tight—so the stitches will slide easily along your needles.

• To get nice borders, always tighten the yarn a little more on the first stitch; this way the knitting won't get too loose.

• To fix a dropped stitch, insert the tip of a crochet hook through the lost stitch, catch the horizontal strand of yarn just above it, and pull it through the stitch. Repeat as many times as there are unraveled rows, then replace the stitch on the left needle.

15

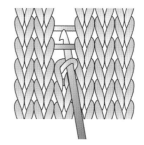

ABBREVIATIONS

We have used the following abbreviations in this book to allow you to quickly and easily read the patterns:

Decrease(s)	dec(s)
Increase(s)	inc(s)
Knit	k
Knit 2 stitches together	k2tog
Make 1	M1
Purl	p
Purl 2 stitches together	p2tog
Repeat	rep
Right side	RS
Round(s)	rnd(s)
Slip, knit, pass	skp
Stitch(es)	st(s)
Wrong side	WS

SKILL LEVEL

✳ *EASY*

✳✳ *INTERMEDIATE*

✳✳✳ *ADVANCED*

A collection of Trendy Shawlettes.

Mademoiselle Sophie's organized chaos.

Karma, the mascot of Breaking the Wool.

Works in progress.

Snowflake Scarf **

White as snow, a scarf for facing winter with beauty and softness.

SIZE
❋ Adult (one size)

MATERIALS
❋ Alpaca-wool blend super bulky weight yarn: 9 skeins white (16 oz./ 450 g; shown in Fonty Pôle, #350)
❋ Size 11 (8 mm) needles
❋ Yarn needle

STITCHES USED
❋ Stockinette stitch
❋ 1 x 1 ribbing
❋ Bobbles

GAUGE
❋ In stockinette stitch with size 11 needles, 4" x 4"/10 x 10 cm = 11 sts x 14 rows

SCARF
Cast on 30 sts. Work in 1 x 1 ribbing for 5½"/14 cm, then work in stockinette stitch until the piece measures 78¾"/200 cm. Finish with 5½"/14 cm 1 x 1 ribbing. Bind off.

POCKETS (MAKE 2)
The pockets are made in stockinette stitch, adding bobbles (see right) at different points, then finishing in 1 x 1 ribbing.

Cast on 19 sts.
Row 1: Knit.
Row 2: Purl.
Row 3: K4, 1 bobble, k4, 1 bobble, k4, 1 bobble, k4.
Row 4: Purl.
Row 5: Knit.
Row 6: Purl.
Row 7: Knit.
Row 8: Purl.
Row 9: K6, 1 bobble, k5, 1 bobble, k6.
Row 10: Purl.
Row 11: Knit.
Row 12: Purl.
Row 13: Knit.
Row 14: Purl.
Row 15: K4, 1 bobble, k4, 1 bobble, k4, 1 bobble, k4.
Row 16: Purl.
Row 17: Knit.
Row 18: Purl.
Row 19: Knit.
Finish with 4 rows of 1 x 1 ribbing. Bind off.

BOBBLES
In the next stitch, work 5 stitches: k1, p1, k1, p1, k1. Turn the work, slip 1 st, and purl the next 4 sts. Turn the work, slip 1 st, and knit the next 4 sts. Turn the work, slip 1 st, p2tog twice. Turn the work one last time and knit the next 3 sts together. Continue as indicated in the pattern.

FINISHING
Sew the pockets to the scarf 8½"/22 cm from each end, centering them widthwise.

TIPS
Stockinette stitch has a tendency to roll up along the edges; to prevent this, block the work by getting it damp and then ironing it with a thin cloth over it.

Little Garter Stitch Beret *

Mother and daughter match with these cute pom-pom berets.

SIZES
❉ Adult (Child 3–4 years)

MATERIALS
❉ 100% wool medium weight yarn: 1½ skeins blue (2.6 oz./75 g; shown in Fonty Aubusson, #20); 2 skeins gray (3.5 oz./100 g; shown in #07)
❉ Size 9 (5.5 mm) (adult) and size 8 (5.0 mm) (child) needles
❉ Yarn needle
❉ 2 cardboard rings, each 2¾"/7 cm in diameter, and a pair of scissors (for the pom-poms)

STITCH USED
❉ Garter stitch

GAUGE
❉ In garter stitch with size 9 (5.5 mm) needles, 4" x 4"/10 x 10 cm = 14 sts x 35 rows (adult); with size 8 (5.0 mm) needles, 4" x 4"/10 x 10 cm = 19 sts x 40 rows (child)

With the size 9 (8) needles, cast on 76 (76) sts and work in garter stitch for 58 (48) rows, about 6¾"/17 cm (5½"/14 cm). Start decreasing as follows.

Dec Row 1: K2, *k2tog, k10 (8); rep from * around, ending with k2.
Knit 2 (2) rows even.
Dec Row 2: K2, *k2tog, k9 (7); rep from * around, ending with k2.
Knit 2 (1) row(s) even.
Dec Row 3: K2, *k2tog, k8 (6); rep from * around, ending with k2.
Knit 2 (1) row(s) even.
Dec Row 4: K2, *k2tog, k7 (5); rep from * around, ending with k2.
Continue decreasing in this pattern, with the decreases always above the previous ones, until 28 (22) sts remain.
Knit 1 row even.
Last Row: K2, *k2tog; rep from * around, ending with k2.
Cut the yarn, leaving a long tail. Use a yarn needle to draw the tail through the remaining stitches to close the top of the hat. With the remaining yarn, sew the side seam of the hat.

POM-POM
Use two rings of cardboard 2¾"/7 cm wide to make a pom-pom, following the instructions on page 26.
Sew the pom-pom to the crown of the hat, weaving in the ends of the yarn to the inside.

Trendy Shawlette **

A classic that can be knotted like a scarf. Wrap it around; that's all there is to it!

SIZES
✢ Adult (Child 3–4 years)

MATERIALS
✢ Alpaca-wool blend super bulky weight yarn: 5 (3) skeins mauve, [8.1 oz./ 230 g (4.9 oz./140 g); shown in Fonty Pôle, #367]
✢ Size 11 (8.0 mm) needles

STITCH USED
✢ Garter stitch

GAUGE
✢ In garter stitch with size 11 (8.0 mm) needles, 4" x 4"/10 x 10 cm = 11 sts x 22 rows

The shawl is knitted in garter stitch, using yarn overs to increase just before the last stitch of each row.

Cast on 4 sts.
Row 1: K4.
Row 2: K3, yo, k1.
Row 3: K4, yo, k1.
Row 4: K5, yo, k1.
Continue in pattern until the piece measures 19¾"/50 cm long from the point of the shawl to the top edge. Bind off.

TASSELS
Cut 10 strands of yarn 15¾"/40 cm (7¾"/20 cm) long and separate them into two bundles of 5 (one for each point). Fold the bundles in half. Use your fingers to pass them through the end stitch on each point, and draw the free ends through the folded loop, tugging gently to secure. (See page 44 for illustrations.)

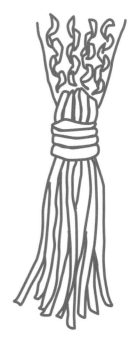

TIPS
Bind off the stitches very loosely so that the scarf will easily go around your neck. This project can be made in any size and with any kind of yarn.

Bow-Tied Mitts *

Bring out these mitts to keep little hands nice and warm.

SIZES
❋ Adult (Child 3–4 years)

MATERIALS
❋ 100% merino wool fine weight yarn: 1 skein light gray (1.8 oz./50 g; shown in Fonty Olympe, #775); .3 oz./10 g pink for the bows (shown in Fonty Olympe, #780)
❋ Lurex (metallic) yarn (.35 oz./10 g)
❋ Size 6 (4.0 mm) and 8 (5.0 mm) needles
❋ Yarn needle

STITCH USED
❋ Garter stitch

GAUGE
❋ In garter stitch with size 8 (5.0 mm) needles, 4" x 4"/10 x 10 cm = 18 sts x 40 rows; with size 6 (4.0 mm) needles, 4" x 4"/10 x 10 cm = 22 sts x 48 rows

MITTS
With the size 6 (4.0 mm) needles, cast on 32 (22) sts. Work in garter stitch for 4"/10 cm (2"/5 cm). Continue with the size 8 (5.0 mm) needles for 3½"/9 cm (2"/5 cm). Bind off.

Sew up the side seam, leaving a 1½"/4 cm (1"/3 cm) opening for the thumb, 1"/3 cm (¾"/2 cm) from the top edge.

Make the second mitt the same way.

BOWS
The bow is made the same for the adult and child sizes.

With the size 8 (5.0 mm) needles, cast on 8 sts and knit 8 rows in garter stitch. Bind off.

Use the metallic yarn to tie off the knitted rectangle in the center, to form a little bow; wind the yarn around and around to create a little sparkly band in the center. Knot the yarn 3 times, then cut off the ends.

Sew the little bow to the right-hand mitt in the desired place.

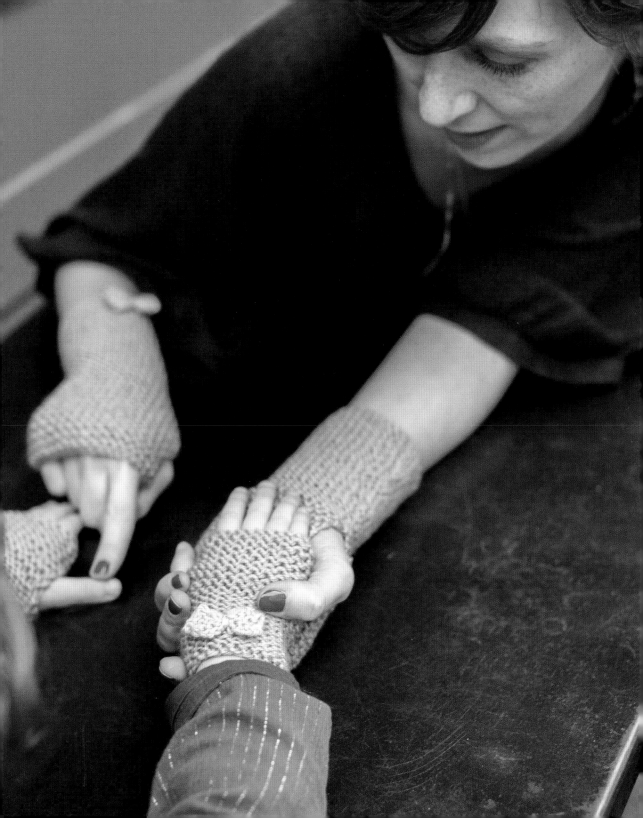

Pom-Pom Hat ✸✸

An angora pom-pom gives a touch of chic to this ultra-simple bonnet.

SIZES
✳ Adult (Child 3–4 years)

MATERIALS
✳ 100% wool super bulky weight yarn: 1 skein royal blue [3.5 oz./100 g (2.8 oz./80 g); shown in Fonty Pacha, #003]
✳ Angora-wool blend fine weight yarn: 1 skein light gray (.9 oz./25 g; shown in Fonty Coeur d'Angora, #211), for the pom-pom
✳ Size 17 (12.75 mm) circular needle (16"/ 40 cm)
✳ 1 ring-style stitch marker
✳ 2 cardboard rings 4⅓"/ 11 cm (2¾"/7 cm) in diameter and a pair of scissors (for the pom-pom)
✳ Yarn needle

STITCH USED
✳ 1 x 1 ribbing

GAUGE
✳ In 1 x 1 ribbing with size 17 (12.75 mm) needles, 4" x 4"/10 x 10 cm = 10 sts x 11 rows

Cast on 40 (32) sts.

Slide the stitch marker onto the needles before the first stitch; this will allow you to identify the beginning of the round.

Work in the round in 1 x 1 ribbing.

When the piece measures about 7¾"/20 cm (4¾"/12 cm) tall, k2tog all the way around for two rounds—10 (8) stitches remaining.

Cut the yarn, pass the end through the remaining stitches, and pull to close the top of the hat. Weave in the ends.

THE POM-POM

Take two cardboard rings 4⅓"/11 cm (2¾"/7 cm) in diameter. Place them on top of each other, then wrap the yarn around the rings and through the middle. Continue until the cardboard is completely covered up.

Slide the blade of the scissors between the two rings to cut the yarn all the way around the outside edge.

Tie a length of yarn tightly around the center of the bundle, between the two rings; fluff out the pom-pom to finish it.

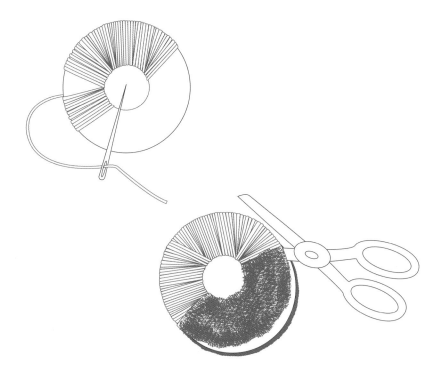

Angora Cowl and Fingerless Gloves *

Bright electric blue + graphic shaping = A perfect ensemble to light up the winter.

SIZES

❊ Adult (Child 3–4 years)

MATERIALS

For the cowl

❊ Angora-wool blend fine weight yarn: 4 (2) skeins blue [3.5 oz./100 g (1.7 oz./50 g); shown in Fonty Coeur d'Angora, #227]

❊ Size 11 (8.0 mm) needles

❊ Size 8 (5.0 mm) needles

❊ Yarn needle

For the gloves

❊ Angora-wool blend fine weight yarn: 1 (1) skein blue [.9 oz./25 g (.3 oz./10 g); shown in Fonty Coeur d'Angora, #227]

STITCHES USED

❊ Garter stitch (with two strands of yarn)

❊ 1 x 1 ribbing (for the gloves)

GAUGES

For the cowl:

❊ In garter stitch with size 11 (8.0 mm) needles and two strands of yarn, 4" x 4"/10 x 10 cm = 13 sts x 22 rows

For the gloves:

❊ In 1 x 1 ribbing with size 8 (5.0 mm) needles, 4" x 4"/10 x 10 cm = 24 sts x 22 rows

COWL

With two strands of yarn, cast on 3 sts.

Row 1: K3.
Row 2: K2, M1, k1.
Row 3: K3, M1, k1.
Row 4: K4, M1, k1.

Continue increasing in this pattern until you have 60 (45) sts. Stop increasing and knit every row even for another 6¼"/16 cm (2"/5 cm).

Loosely bind off.

Use the yarn needle to sew the straight sides together for the back neck seam. Weave in the ends.

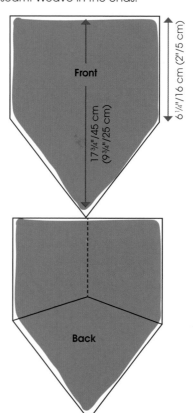

Front

17¾"/45 cm (9¾"/25 cm)

6¼"/16 cm (2"/5 cm)

Back

FINGERLESS GLOVES

Cast on 32 (22) sts. Work in 1 x 1 ribbing until the piece measures 11¾"/30 cm (6"/15 cm) long. Bind off and sew the side seam, leaving an opening 1½"/4 cm (1"/3 cm) long for the thumb, 1"/3 cm (¾"/2 cm) from the top edge.

Weave in the ends.

Diamond Wrap **

For the most patient knitters: A gorgeous stole in seed stitch, enhanced with a diamond design.

SIZE
❋ Adult (one size)

MATERIALS
❋ Alpaca-wool blend super bulky weight yarn:
  11 skeins dark gray (19.4 oz./550 g; shown in Fonty Pôle, #378)
❋ Size 13 (9.0 mm) needles
❋ Yarn needle

STITCHES USED
❋ Seed stitch
❋ Diamond pattern

GAUGE
❋ In seed stitch with size 13 (9.0 mm) needles,
  4" x 4"/10 x 10 cm = 24 sts x 15 rows

Cast on 55 sts. Work in seed stitch for 1½"/4 cm.

Start the diamond pattern, keeping a border of seed stitch on each side (see the chart on page 33).

Row 1: K1, p1, k1, *k6, k2tog, yo, k1, yo, k2tog, k5; repeat from * across to last 4 sts, k1, p1, k1, p1.

Row 2 and every even-numbered row: P1, k1, p1, purl to last 3 sts, k1, p1, k1.

Row 3: K1, p1, k1, *k5, k2tog, yo, k3, yo, k2tog, k4; repeat from * across to last 4 sts, k1, p1, k1, p1.

Row 5: K1, p1, k1, *k4, k2tog, yo, k5, yo, k2tog, k3; repeat from * across to last 4 sts, k1, p1, k1, p1.

Row 7: K1, p1, k1, * k3, k2tog, yo, k7, yo, k2tog, k2; repeat from * across to last 4 sts, k1, p1, k1, p1.

Row 9: K1, p1, k1, *k2, k2tog, yo, k9, yo, k2tog, k1; repeat from * across to last 4 sts, k1, p1, k1, p1.

Row 11: K1, p1, k1, *k1, k2tog, yo, k11 yo, k2tog; repeat from * across to last 4 sts, k1, p1, k1, p1.

Row 13: K1, p1, k1, *k1, yo, k2tog, k11, k2tog, yo; repeat from * across to last 4 sts, k1, p1, k1, p1.

Row 15: K1, p1, k1, *k2, yo, k2tog, k9, k2tog, yo, k1; repeat from * across to last 4 sts, k1, p1, k1, p1.

Row 17: K1, p1, k1, *k3, yo, k2tog, k7, k2tog, yo, k2; repeat from * across to last 4 sts, k1, p1, k1, p1.

Row 19: K1, p1, k1, *k4, yo, k2tog, k5, k2tog, yo, k3; repeat from * across to last 4 sts, k1, p1, k1, p1.

Row 21: K1, p1, k1, *k5, yo, k2tog, k3, k2tog, yo, k4; repeat from * across to last 4 sts, k1, p1, k1, p1.

Row 23: K1, p1, k1, *k6, yo, k2tog, k1, k2tog, yo, k5; repeat from * across to last 4 sts, k1, p1, k1, p1.

Row 25: K1, p1, k1, knit to last 4 sts, k1, p1, k1, p1.

Continue in seed stitch until the piece measures 49¼"/125 cm long in all, then repeat the diamond pattern for the opposite border.

Finish with 1½"/4 cm of seed stitch, then bind off loosely.

Weave in the ends.

* Diamond pattern *

Row 25
Row 23
Row 21
Row 19
Row 17
Row 15
Row 13
Row 11
Row 9
Row 7
Row 5
Row 3
Row 1

24
22
20
18
16
14
12
10
8
6
4
2

23 22 21 20 19 18 17 16 15 14 13 12 11 10 9 8 7 6 5 4 3 2 1

	RS: knit WS: purl
	RS: purl WS: knit
o	yarn over
⟋	knit 2 stitches together

Lace Scarf ✳✳✳

Light as a feather, this scarf will wrap delicately around your neck.

SIZE
✳ Adult (one size)

MATERIALS
✳ Wool-mohair blend fine weight yarn: 2 skeins dusty rose (3.9 oz./110 g; shown in Fonty Ombelle, #1049)
✳ Size 9 (5.5 mm) needles
✳ Yarn needle

STITCH USED
✳ Lace pattern

GAUGE
✳ In lace pattern with size 9 (5.5 mm) needles, 4" x 4"/10 x 10 cm = 20 sts x 19 rows

Cast on 53 stitches. Knit 2 rows even. Start lace pattern.

Row 1: K1, *yo, skp, k8; repeat from * to last 2 sts, k2.

Row 2 and every even-numbered row: Purl.

Row 3: K1, *k1, yo, skp, k5, k2tog, yo; repeat from * to last 2 sts, k2.

Row 5: K1, *k2, yo, skp, k3, k2tog, yo, k1; repeat from * to last 2 sts, k2.

Row 7: K1, *k5, yo, skp, k3; repeat from * to last 2 sts, k2.

Row 9: K1, *k3, k2tog, yo, k1, yo, skp, k2; repeat from * to last 2 sts, k2.

Repeat the 10 rows of the lace pattern until the piece measures 59"/150 cm long, then finish with 2 rows of knit. Bind off.

TIP

For a nice finished look, block your work by ironing the scarf on low heat (see page 15).

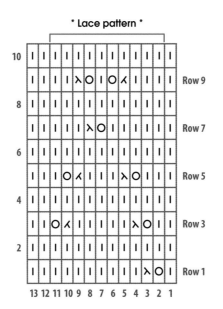

* Lace pattern *

13 12 11 10 9 8 7 6 5 4 3 2 1

☐	RS: knit WS: purl
⊟	RS: purl WS: knit
○	yarn over
⊠	slip, knit, pass
⊿	knit 2 stitches together

Reversible Hat **

A classic and timeless hat that will fit any head!

SIZES

❋ One size. The ribbing makes this hat super stretchy, and the brim can be folded, making this hat fit nearly any size.

MATERIALS

❋ Merino wool medium weight yarn: I skein blue (1.8 oz./50 g; shown in Bergère de France Pur Mérinos Français, #291-481)
❋ Size 8 (5.0 mm) circular needles (16"/40 cm)
❋ I ring-style stitch marker
❋ Yarn needle

STITCH USED

❋ 2 x 2 ribbing: *knit 2, purl 2; rep from * around

GAUGE

❋ In 2 x 2 ribbing with size 8 (5.0 mm) needle: 4" x 4"/10 x 10 cm = 28 sts x 24 rows

The stitch marker allows you to identify the beginning of the round.

Cast on 76 sts. Slide the stitch marker onto the needle before the first stitch.

Work in the round in 2 x 2 ribbing for 58 rnds, about 9"/23 cm (7¾"/20 cm).

On the next rnd, begin decreasing: *k2tog, p2tog; repeat from * around—38 sts remaining.

Work 3 rnds in 2 x 2 ribbing.

In the next rnd, finish decreasing by knitting 2 sts together all the way around.

Knit 1 rnd.

Cut the yarn, leaving a tail of about 11¾"/30 cm, and thread the end through the remaining stitches. Draw tight to close the top of the hat, then weave in the end.

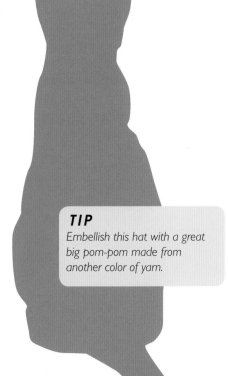

TIP

Embellish this hat with a great big pom-pom made from another color of yarn.

Love Cowl *

A super soft yarn, a bright color: you'll love to wrap yourself in this cozy cowl.

SIZE
* Adult (one size)

MATERIALS
* Alpaca fine weight yarn: 4 skeins red (6.3 oz./ 180 g; shown in Fonty Alpaga, #759)
* Size 6 (4.0 mm) circular needles (32"/80 cm)
* Yarn needle

STITCH USED
* Stockinette stitch on circular needles: knit all stitches every round

GAUGE
* In stockinette stitch with size 6 (4.0 mm) needles, 4" x 4"/10 x 10 cm = 20 sts x 32 rows

Cast on 180 sts. Knit in the round for 15¾"/40 cm (128 rows); this will produce stockinette stitch.
Bind off very loosely and weave in the ends.

Scarf with Frills *

There's a pretty simplicity in this pale blue color. Here, it's the ruffle that makes the style!

SIZES
❊ Adult (Child 3–4 years)

MATERIALS
❊ Extra fine alpaca-merino blend bulky weight yarn: 10 (5) skeins light blue [17.75 oz./500 g (8.8 oz./250 g); shown in Fonty Boréal, #710]
❊ Size 10½ (6.5 mm) needles
❊ Yarn needle

STITCHES USED
❊ Garter stitch
❊ Stockinette stitch

GAUGE
❊ In garter stitch with size 10½ (6.5 mm) needles, 4" x 4"/10 x 10 cm = 14 sts x 26 rows

Cast on 80 (40) sts.

Rows 1 to 11: Start to make the ruffle: Work 3 rows in garter stitch. Work the next 8 rows in stockinette stitch, starting with a purl row (then a knit row).

Row 12: K2tog across—40 (20) sts remaining.

Row 13: Purl.

Continue in garter stitch until the whole piece measures 67"/170 cm (31½"/80 cm). In the next row, work an M1 increase in between each pair of stitches to return to 80 (40) sts.

Work 9 rows in stockinette stitch, then 3 rows in garter stitch.

Bind off.

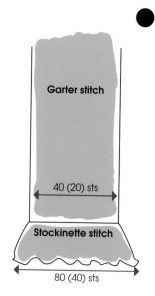

Garter stitch

40 (20) sts

Stockinette stitch

80 (40) sts

Ear-Warming Headband *

The indispensable winter accessory. Here, a little touch of metallic yarn brings out your glamorous side.

SIZES
❉ Adult (Child 3–4 years)

MATERIALS
❉ Merino wool medium
 weight yarn: 1 skein rust
 (1.8 oz./50 g; shown in
 Bergère de France Pur
 Mérinos Français, Brique)
❉ Lurex (metallic) yarn
 (.3 oz/10 g)
❉ Size 8 (5.0 mm) needles
❉ Yarn needle

STITCH USED
❉ 1 x 1 ribbing

GAUGE
❉ In 1 x 1 ribbing with size
 8 (5.0 mm) needles,
 4" x 4"/10 x 10 cm =
 25 sts x 20 rows

Cast on 20 sts. Work in 1 x 1 ribbing for 15¾"/40 cm (13¾"/35 cm). Bind off. Sew the narrow ends of the piece together, using the yarn needle. Use your hands to gather the band at the seam and wrap a length of metallic yarn (or yarn in the same color) around it to hide the seam and to add a little sparkly band. Weave in the ends.

TIP
To make headbands for mountain trips or for when it's really cold, use thick yarn.

Striped Scarf *

Simple stitches and natural colors: A perfect combination for a refined scarf.

SIZES
❋ Adult (Child 3–4 years)

MATERIALS
❋ 100% wool medium weight
  yarn: 3 (2) skeins gray
  [4.6 oz./130 g (2.8 oz./
  80 g); shown in Bergère de
  France Mouton, Gris
  Mélèze—Larch Gray];
  3 (2) skeins white
  [4.2 oz./120 g. (2.8 oz./
  80 g; shown in Blanc
  Mouton—Sheep White]
❋ Size 10 (6.0 mm) needles
❋ Yarn needle

STITCH USED
❋ Garter stitch

GAUGE
❋ In garter stitch with size
  10 (6.0 mm) needles,
  4" x 4"/10 x 10 cm =
  17 sts x 30 rows

Cast on 25 sts with white yarn. Knit 4 rows with white, then 4 rows with gray, then another 4 rows in white, and finally 4 rows in gray. Continue with the white yarn for 17¾"/45 cm (6"/15 cm).
Change to the gray yarn and knit until the piece measures 49¼"/125 cm (9½"/50 cm) in all. Change back to white and knit for another 17¾"/45 cm (6"/15 cm).
Knit 4 rows gray, 4 rows white, 4 rows gray, and 4 rows white.
Bind off all the stitches.

FRINGE
Cut two strands of white yarn 7¾"/20 cm (4"/10 cm) long. Holding the strands together, fold them in half, then pass the folded end through an edge stitch on one narrow end of the scarf. Put your fingers through this loop, grab the cut ends of the strands, and pull them gently through to form one section of fringe.
Add 25 sections of fringe in this way to each end of the scarf.

TIP
The ends of yarn at each color change can be taken up in the first stitches of the next row for a smooth finish.

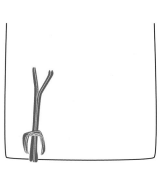

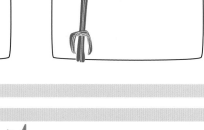

Emerald Shawlette *

Pick fuzzy yarn in a bright color for this soft, gorgeous shawlette.

SIZES
✳ Adult S (M, L)
✳ Child 3–4 years: see
   sidebar below

MATERIALS
✳ Mohair-acrylic-nylon blend
   super bulky weight yarn:
   2 skeins emerald green
   (7 oz./200 g; shown in
   Rico Fashion Gigantic
   Mohair, Emerald)
✳ Size 17 (12.75 mm)
   needles
✳ Silver Lurex (metallic) yarn
   (.3 oz./10 g)
✳ Sewing needle
✳ Yarn needle
✳ Button, 1"/3 cm in
   diameter

STITCH USED
✳ Garter stitch

GAUGE
✳ In garter stitch with size
   17 (12.75 mm) needles,
   4" x 4"/10 x 10 cm =
   7 sts x 14 rows

This scarf is a simple rectangle knit in garter stitch.

Cast on 50 (55, 60) sts and work in garter stitch until the piece measures 15¾"/40 cm long.
Bind off the sts and weave in the ends.

BOW
Cast on 7 sts.
Work in garter stitch until the piece measures about 5"/13 cm, then bind off.
Wrap the metallic yarn around the middle of the rectangle to form a bow shape. Wrap both ends of the yarn around several times to create a little sparkly band.
Knot the ends together 3 times, then trim them.

FINISHING
Sew the bow to the top right corner of the shawlette.
Sew a button to the top left corner of the rectangle, 2¾"/7 cm from the left edge and 4"/10 cm from the top.
To attach the shawlette around your neck, just slip the button through the stitches of the opposite side; the bow will hide the button.

CHILD SIZE (3–4 YEARS)
Use 1 skein of yarn. Cast on 45 sts and work in garter stitch until the piece measures 8½"/22 cm in all. Bind off and weave in the ends. To make the bow, cast on 6 sts and knit for 2¼"/6 cm. Follow the rest of the instructions just as for the adult sizes.

Knotted Scarf *

The bow creates the style; all you have to do is play with the colors!

SIZES
✳ Adult (Child 3–4 years)

MATERIALS
✳ Alpaca-wool blend super bulky weight yarn: 1 skein forest green (1.8 oz./50 g; shown in Fonty Pôle, #363); 1 skein light green (1.8 oz. 50 g; shown in #349)
✳ Size 13 (9.0 mm) needles
✳ Yarn needle

STITCHES USED
✳ Garter stitch
✳ Seed stitch

GAUGE
✳ In garter stitch with size 13 (9.0 mm) needles, 4" x 4"/10 x 10 cm = 12 sts x 18 rows
✳ In seed stitch with size 13 (9.0 mm) needles, 4" x 4"/10 x 10 cm = 12 sts x 15 rows

48

With the light green yarn, cast on 9 sts and work in seed stitch for 17¾"/45 cm (14"/36 cm).
Change to forest green yarn and begin increasing:
Row 1: K1, M1, k7, M1, k1.
Row 2: K1, M1, k9, M1, k1.
You should have 13 sts at this point. Stop increasing here for the child size, or continue increasing until you have 19 sts for the adult size.
Continue in garter stitch with forest green yarn for 13¾"/35 cm (11¾"/30 cm).

Change to the light green yarn and knit 1 row.
Begin decreasing:
Row 1: K1, k2tog, k13 (9), k2tog, k1.
Row 2: K1, k2tog, k11 (7), k2tog, k1.
Decrease until you are back to the original 9 sts (both sizes).
Continue in seed stitch for 17¾"/ 45 cm (14"/36 cm).
Bind off the sts and weave in the ends.

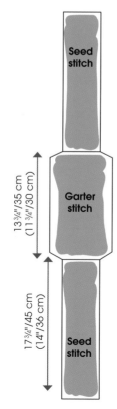

Seed stitch

Garter stitch

Seed stitch

13¾"/35 cm (11¾"/30 cm)

17¾"/45 cm (14"/36 cm)

Cloud Scarf ✳✳

The bows add a touch of whimsy to this otherwise sober scarf.

SIZE
✳ *Adult*
✳ *Child 3–4 years: see sidebar below*

MATERIALS
✳ *100% wool fine weight yarn: 3 skeins light gray (5.3 oz./150 g; shown in Fonty Ambiance, #329)*
✳ *Size 8 (5.0 mm) needles*
✳ *Yarn needle*

STITCHES USED
✳ *Cloud stitch: a combination of knit and purl stitches*
✳ *Garter stitch (bows)*

GAUGE
✳ *In stockinette stitch with size 8 (5.0 mm) needles, 4" x 4"/10 x 10 cm = 20 sts x 28 rows*

Cast on 38 sts.
Work in garter stitch for 4 rows.
Row 1: Knit.
Row 2: K3, purl to last 3 sts, k3.
Row 3: K3, *k3, p1; repeat from * to last 3 sts, k3.
Row 4: K3, purl to last 3 sts, k3.
Row 5: Knit.
Row 6: K3, purl to last 3 sts, k3.
Row 7: K4, *p1, k3; repeat from * to last 6 sts, p1, k5.
Row 8: K3, purl to last 3 sts, k3.
Repeat these 8 rows until the piece measures about 59"/150 cm long.
Work in garter stitch for 4 rows. Bind off loosely.
Weave in the ends.

CHILD SIZE (3–4 YEARS)
Use 2 skeins of yarn. Follow the same instructions as for the adult size, but make the scarf 30"/75 cm long instead of 59"/150 cm.

BOWS
Cast on 14 sts.
Work in garter stitch until the piece measures 5½"/14 cm. Bind off loosely.
Use a strand of yarn to tie the piece in the middle to form a bow.
Sew the bow to the end of the scarf, about 4"/10 cm from the bottom edge, centering it widthwise on the scarf.

TIP
Make the bow in another color of yarn for a more creative version.

Fuschia Cowl **

The combination of mohair and Liberty fabric gives a crazy allure to the most basic of outfits.

SIZE

❉ Adult (Child 3–4 years)

MATERIALS

❉ Mohair-wool blend fine weight yarn: 2 (1) skeins fuchsia [3.9 oz./110 g (1.8 oz./50 g); shown in Fonty Ombelle, #1038]

❉ Size 17 (12.75 mm) needles

❉ Bias tape from Liberty fabric or other strip of fabric, 39"/1 m

STITCH USED

❉ 1 x 1 ribbing

GAUGE

❉ In 1 x 1 ribbing with size 17 (12.75 mm) needles, 4" x 4"/10 x 10 cm = 10 sts x 10 rows

This cowl is a rectangle worked in 1 x 1 ribbing, knit with two strands of yarn.

Cast on 22 (12) sts. Work in 1 x 1 ribbing until the piece measures about 17¾"/45 cm. Bind off. Weave in ends.
Pass the strip of Liberty fabric through the stitches on either end of the cowl, so that you can close it at the top.
Form a pretty loop.

Strip of Liberty fabric

Camel Beanie **

A fashion classic that goes well with any style.

SIZES
❋ Adult (Child 3–4 years)

MATERIALS
❋ 100% camel-hair medium weight yarn: 1 skein camel color (1.8 oz./50 g; shown in Fonty Camel, #2)
❋ Size 9 (5.5 mm) circular needles (16"/40 cm)
❋ Yarn needle
❋ Ring-style stitch marker

STITCHES USED
❋ 2 x 2 ribbing: *knit 2, purl 2; rep from * around
❋ Stockinette stitch in the round: knit all stitches every round

GAUGE
❋ In stockinette stitch with size 9 (5.5 mm) needles, 4" x 4"/10 x 10 cm = 24 sts x 32 rows

Cast on 90 (60) sts. Join to work in the round, placing marker for start of round.

Work in 2 x 2 ribbing (k2, p2 around) for 1"/3 cm.

Knit 18 (11) rows, about 3"/8 cm (2"/5 cm).

Next round: K2tog around—45 (30) sts remaining.

Knit even for 4"/10 cm more.

Next round: K2tog around—23 (15) sts.

Cut the yarn, leaving an 11¾"/30 cm tail, and pass the tail through the remaining sts. Pull tight. Weave in ends.

TIP

You can work the simple border in 1 x 1 ribbing for 1"/3 cm to give your hat a more traditional look.

Cashmere Headband *

This evening accessory will charm you with its softness and color.

SIZE
✳ Adult (one size)

MATERIALS
✳ Cashmere-silk-wool blend
    lace weight yarn: 1 skein
    blue-green (.9 oz./25 g;
    shown in Filatura Di Crosa
    Superior, #55)
✳ Extra fine merino wool
    lace weight yarn: 1 skein
    blue-green (.9 oz./25 g;
    shown in Filatura Di Crosa
    Nirvana, #7)
✳ Size 8 (5.0 mm) needles
✳ Yarn needle

STITCH USED
✳ Garter stitch

GAUGE
✳ In garter stitch with size
    8 (5.0 mm) needles,
    4" x 4"/10 x 10 cm =
    20 sts x 34 rows

Holding both yarns together, cast on
    18 sts.
Work 2 rows in garter stitch.
Row 3: K2, *yo, k2tog, k2; repeat from *
    across to last 4 sts, k2, yo, k2—19 sts.
Work 3 rows in garter stitch.
Row 9: K2, yo, k2tog, k11, k2tog, yo, k2.
Row 10: Knit.
Repeat Rows 9 and 10 until the piece
    measures 39¼"/100 cm in all.
Next Row: K2, *yo, k2tog, k2; repeat from
    * across to last 4 sts, k2, yo, k2.
Work 2 rows in garter stitch.
Bind off loosely. Weave in ends.

XXL Scarf **

You're guaranteed to make a big impact with this maxi scarf in an audacious shade of mustard yellow!

SIZE
❊ Adult (one size)

MATERIALS
❊ Wool-acrylic blend super bulky weight yarn: 4 skeins mustard yellow (14 oz./ 400 g; shown in Katia North, #83)
❊ Size 17 (12.75 mm) needles
❊ Yarn needle

STITCH USED
❊ Stitch pattern: uses knit, purl, slip, and yarn over

GAUGE
❊ In stitch pattern with size 17 (12.75 mm) needles, 4" x 4"/10 x 10 cm = 8 sts x 10 rows

Cast on 17 sts.

Row 1: P2, *k3, p2; repeat from * across.

Row 2: K2, *p3, k2; repeat from * across.

Row 3: P2, *sl 1 as if to purl, k1, yo, k1, pass slipped stitch over these 3 sts, p2; repeat from * across.

Row 4: K2, *p3, k2; repeat from * across.

Repeat these 4 rows until the piece measures 78¾"/200 cm (or the desired length) in all. Bind off the stitches and weave in the ends.

Silver Border Beret **

A strand of metallic yarn added to the wool gives this hat a touch of flirtiness and elegance.

SIZES
❊ Adult (Child 3–4 years)

MATERIALS
❊ 100% wool fine weight yarn: I skein light gray (1.8 oz./50g; shown in Fonty Ambience, #329)
❊ Size 8 (5.0 mm) needles
❊ Silver Lurex (metallic) yarn (.3 oz./10 g)
❊ Yarn needle

STITCH USED
❊ Garter stitch

GAUGE
❊ In garter stitch with size 8 (5.0 mm) needles, 4" x 4"/10 x 10 cm = 17 sts x 40 rows

With 1 strand each of wool and metallic yarn held together, cast on 76 sts.

Work in garter stitch for 9 rows (about ¾"/2 cm).

Drop metallic yarn and continue in wool alone for 36 more rows, about 5½"/14 cm (4¾"/12 cm).

Decrease Row 1: *K2tog, k1; repeat from * to last st, k1—51 sts remaining.

Decrease Row 2: *K2tog, k1; repeat from * across—34 sts remaining.

Next Row: Knit.

Decrease Row 3: *K2tog, k1; repeat from * to last st, k1—23 sts remaining.

Decrease Row 4: *K2tog, k1; repeat from * to last 2 sts, k2tog—15 sts remaining.

Decrease Row 5: *K2tog, k1; repeat from * across—10 sts remaining.

Next Row: Knit.

Cut the yarn, leaving a long tail. Use a yarn needle to pass the tail through the remaining stitches and pull tight. Sew up the back seam of the hat with the tail. Weave in the ends.

TIP
For the child version, decorate this beret with a little bow like the ones used on the fingerless mitts on page 24.

Pom-Pom Mittens **

Knit from beautiful soft yarn, these mittens are just as suited for Mamas as for little ones.

LEFT MITTEN

With the size 7 (4.5 mm) needles, cast on 32 (22) sts.

Work in 1 x 1 ribbing for 4"/10 cm (1½"/4 cm), to form the cuff of the mitten.

Continue with the size 8 (5.0 mm) needles in stockinette stitch.

Knit 1 row.

Next Row: Purl the first 13 (8) sts, place a stitch marker, p3, place the second marker, then purl the remaining 16 (11) sts.

Work 2 rows even in stockinette stitch, slipping the stitch markers from needle to needle as you reach them.

Increase Row 1: K13 (8), slip marker, M1, k3, M1, slip marker, k to end.

Work 3 rows even in stockinette stitch.

Increase Row 2: K to first marker, slip marker, M1, k5, M1, slip marker, k to end.

Purl 1 row.

For the adult size, continue in this pattern, alternating increase rows and 3 stockinette rows, until you have 11 sts between the markers. For the child size, continue until you have 7 stitches between the markers. These 11 (7) sts will form the thumb.

Work the next row until the end of the 11 (7) thumb sts, M1 (you can remove the stitch marker now). Turn the work and work back only across the thumb stitches (you can remove the second stitch marker). Turn again and work 1 increase.

Work back and forth in stockinette stitch on these 13 (9) sts until the thumb measures 2½"/6.5 cm (1"/3 cm) from the base.

Next Row: K1, *k2tog; repeat from * to end.

Cut the yarn, leaving a tail of about 11¾"/30 cm (7¾"/20 cm) to use to sew up the thumb seam. Use a yarn needle to pass this end through all the remaining sts on the needle to close up the top of the thumb, then sew up the side seam. The thumb is finished.

Join the yarn again at the base of the thumb, and pick up 2 new stitches at the base of the thumb to close up the space between the two halves of the mitten body. Finish the row normally.

Continue in stockinette stitch for 4"/10 cm (1½"/4 cm).

Next Row: K1, skp, k10 (5), k2tog, k1, skp, k10 (5), k2tog, k1.

Purl the next row.

Next Row: K1, skp, k8 (3), k2tog, k1, skp, k8 (3), k2tog, k1.

Purl next row.

Next Row: K1, skp, k6 (1), k2tog, k1, skp, k6 (1), k2tog, k1.

Purl next row.

Next Row: K1, skp, *k2tog; repeat from * to end.

Purl next row.

Adult size only:

Next Row: K1, skp, *k2tog; repeat from * to last st, k1.

Purl next row.

Next Row: K1, skp, *k2tog; repeat from * to end.

Purl next row.

HAPPY WOOL

Both sizes:
Cut the yarn, leaving a tail about 15¾"/40 cm (7¾"/20 cm) long. Use a yarn needle to pass the tail through the remaining sts to close up the top of the mitten, pull tight, then sew up the side seam of the mitten.

Weave in the ends. Make the pom-pom (see page 26) and sew it onto the mitten.

RIGHT MITTEN

The right mitten is knitted in the same way as the left mitten; the only difference is the dividing of the stitches to form the thumb: Purl the first 16 (11) sts, place marker, p3, place second marker, purl remaining 13 (8) sts.

TIP
Increase or reduce the size of the thumb and the hand of the mitten to fit your hand.

64

A book, like a life, is a collective adventure. You would be holding nothing but air between your hands if certain people hadn't been at my side. It is an honor to thank them.

Thank you to the whole team at Temps Apprivoisé, who did remarkable work—particularly to Anne-Sophie and Isabelle, for their faith in me, their honesty, and their unflagging enthusiasm.

Thank you to Carole Greffrath, conflict mediator!

Thank you to Claire and Sonia, our inspiring photographer and stylist, who captured the essence of my work with delicacy and sensitivity.

Thank you to Fonty (www.fonty.fr) and Bergère de France (www.bergeredefrance.com) for their benevolence and generosity.

Thank you to the Breaking the Wool (www.breakingthewool.com) team, especially to Julie for her invaluable support and her daily commitment.

Thank you to Karma and her soothing purring.

Thank you to my husband, who put up with living in the middle of wool and who encourages me in my craziest ideas. Thank you to Maman, unconditional fan and wise counselor.

And thank you to my daughter, this joy who is growing up too fast, and to whom I dedicate this book.

Thank you also to: Chez les voisins (vintage products and decor), www.chezlesvoisins.fr; Caroline Gayral, for the rug (p. 23); Tournicote (www.lisenncabane.canalblog.com), for the little decorated stones (p. 24); Rose Miniscule (www.roseminuscule.com) for the doll (p. 11).